...139, 2.

139 Pages of Pining 2.

<u>(aka 139 Pages of Whining.)</u>

Brody McVittie

Table of Contents

The Ones to Get You

You walked into a room full of people..	8
Older Indiscretions, Newer Consequences	9
Okay, you win, but	12
Inappropriate	13
More than mom likes whiskey	15
Mehrabian's Rule	16
This one is about tattoos ... kinda	18
...more than that toy when I was six	20
You'd look good in the passenger seat ...	21
The one about that thing I got you for your birthday	22
The realest shit I've ever wrote	23
Being sick as a kid sucks	24
Always did like playing games	25
Stairs, and shit	27
Seven Seasons	28
Protective	29
You're better to stay away	30
Interlude	31

The Ones to Keep You

This section is decidedly smaller	33
7 & 7	34
7 & 9	35
You're Double-Stuffed Oreos	38
Us, by the numbers	39
"Does this make my ass look fat?"	40
Chicken Soup	41
Saturdays are for	42
Sundays are for	43
Your clothes are on the floor	44
Favorite and Four-letter Word	45
I'm an acquired taste	46
I'm Bi-Polar, maybe	47
Hotel hallways, week analogies	48
You should have been a boxer	49
If relationships are like fights	50
I'm no good for you	51
This will end violently	52
Pedestals are prisons	54
"Ten Things I Don't Deserve!"	55
You're distractingly pretty and suitcase small	56
I guess that's why they call it the blues	58
I like spending time with you	59
What happens when wine	60

Editors and English Teachers.................... 61
You're four feet, one hundred miles 62
I like you more than sushi 63
Interlude 64

The Ones to Lose You

For such a cute voice 67
I like you more 68
You're on your way out the door 69
Mine 70
Tiny Eventualities 71
I hurl words like weapons 73
You woulda been perfect 74
AZ 75
I'm fucking you 77
I messed up 78
80 Pages in, ... 80
You're better than me 81
I'm losing you on rerun 82
Roses to Rust 83
Little Johnny Reiner 84
Tell your parents 85
I'm at least every cliché 86
Because 'Gilbert' isn't a sexy town name   88
You don't fall 90

...in light of explanations, here's one that hurts	92
I create monsters	93
Weekends go by	94
I'll miss the nights	95
Here's a hint	96
I'm over	97
Patterns are for shirts	98
I wrote four of these	99
Losing you is the only thing worse	100
I play with fire	101
Gambling isn't good to me	102
As if	103
Yeah, you're the best I'll ever have	104
I don't miss the hair	105
"Don't Let Me Push You Away"	106
Suadade	107
Tell me	108
I'd rather	110
In your life	111
Today I almost threw out	112
In your defense	113
I thought about you once	114
Interlude	115

The Ones About Me

Of All the Irrational Animals	117
Inconsistently awful	118
I write volumes	119
I've been writing more	120
I'm worse on weekends	121
I need Jesus	123
Despair and Determination	124
Irascible, but justifiably so	125
Dressing pretty	127
Motivation	128
My Momma's Not Gonna Like This One	129
I go for girls	130
I'm on my Marcus Aurelius shit	131
I'm less about half-naked selfies	132
So can we call these lyrics?	133
My Daddy isn't overly proud of me	134
I'm suicidal before coffee	135
If my books are albums, then this shit is an EP	136
Friends and family members	137
138 Pages of Pining	138
Last One	139

The Ones to Get You

You walked into a room full of people

looked at me last

with a look that said you put me first

--so I blame the entirety of the following,
in spirit if not historical fact

on you and your instigating little
eyeballs.

Older Indiscretions, Newer Consequences

Sorry if I'm aggressive

Bully on a Grade Six playground

Maybe you bring out the worse

aspects of an already for-wear

personality

But you have to understand

being around you is two-dollar steak

So tough

Like that math test back then

that made recess so volatile

Hiding anxieties and marbles

Stolen like the kisses I'm trying to

Too many years, and no better off.
I'm tired of counting colors in eyes
just north of lips I can't taste

Watching you and wanting
you watching and wanting, too

Wasting wonderfully
running out of time and the chances time
both brings and takes

Taking it out on each other with words
better saved
Spoken loudly from mouths
better suited
For anything other than the everything

we're spending all our wasted time

not doing

<u>Okay, you win, but...</u>

So I can't get your number

And I can't get you to stay

And I can't get you to admit what we both already know is true

You tell me I can't have it all

Or anything, at all

So can you please, do me one kindness before you go?

Pick up this book, and point to a word that you don't feel

A verse you can't understand

A line that isn't about you.

Inappropriate

Is what you call me

And us

And my intentions

Throwing words into your coffee cup

Swallowing blonde roast and the words you won't

Invitation

And please

And more

Hanging your head on circumstance and
mistrust and other adjectives that matter
as much as the rest of the words you don't
speak when your lips are busy against mine
and between sips that only taste half as
good.

I like you

more than mom likes whiskey

Mehrabian's Rule

My boy Albert famously said

Only seven percent of communication is verbal

--and I'm thankful, because that's the part you suck at

Wasting words like "shouldn't" and "can't" and "fuck, I'd never trust you"

He tells me thirty-eight percent is voice and tone

--and I'm thankful, because you're good at that

Flirtations in whispers and acknowledgements, like "yes, under different circumstances"

But the part you kill

is the *fifty-five percent* body language

Speaking in tongues and fluently
Punching with pheromones and frequently

Telling me without telling me
What my boy Albert already knows
That, despite your thinly-veiled resistance

Us

Is a matter of time

and

Only.

<u>This one is about tattoos
...kinda.</u>

...but it's really about you, too.

There's room on my sleeve

(--not much)

For you to scar me permanently the

way you kinda already have

Looking like you look and leaving like you

Leave

And me to nights with nothing but the stories tattooed onto my arms

Holding whiskey instead of

And hoping the pen can scratch something

Worth the needle I'd let you hold

Leaving something that promises to

Stay

A little longer than you tend to.

I want you

<u>more than that toy when I was six.</u>

The one I prayed for

to a God I haven't believed in

Since that prayer came true.

And if I only get one,

I'll go back and tell that six year old

hold off on that toy

the next one you want

more than anything in the whole wide world

will be worth the next thirty-one years without.

<u>You look good in the passenger seat</u>
Stealing away to some/anywhere

Away from the here
I'm chained to and you're
young enough to
believe you're not
and maybe might
not be.

And

You're the kind I'd
even let control the music

Relinquishing more than I'd like to

Adding miles to the too many I've got

Taking my eyes off the road and
figuring maybe I've got one last
story to tell

Lost on some back road

The way we've been trying to

The one about that thing I got you for your birthday

You wanted a knife for your birthday

--because you're that kind of girl and why not

and because it's not the kind of thing you'd ask the person you pretend to love for

--because he's not that kind of guy and can't be.

So the gifts with the ability to cut come from me

and maybe it's metaphor for the kind of thing we have and can't help

danger on edges, black polished steel and engravings

carved into surfaces, setting something in steel

and as real as the blood from that first cut.

<u>The realest shit I've ever wrote</u>

is the shit I've yet to write about you.

<u>Being sick as a kid sucks.</u>

I came into this world ugly

And so I handle things the same

And meningitis couldn't kill me

The way that girl tried back then

So it's ugly but it works, somehow

And I'm still here

Although I apologize for the way this starts

I can try my damndest to see it doesn't end that way

If you'll wait me out

The way catastrophic childhood diseases

And homicidal exes couldn't.

Always did like playing games

You're my latest last chance at being happy

So congrats on that

The new Super Mario Bros. when I was seven

The new boobs at fifteen

First house at twenty-three

And I'm older, yeah, but I still have one more run

Towards and not the other way

Because being happy is more important

Than being successful or well-off or even doing well

Being happy is all I've got left to chase

And so

tag,

you're it.

Stairs, and shit.

You're at the top of a staircase

And not just metaphorically

And you're not supposed to be calling me to you

So I'm climbing stairs

Literally

Overcoming all of your tiny resistances with every step

Hoping the top is worth the work

Wearing out the soles of shoes

Better suited for the way down

That's waiting on the other side of you.

Seven Seasons.

You smell like hibiscus

And other things that are fun to say and hard to spell

Easily in the *'Top Three Most Enticing Things About You!'*

right under

your eyes

and everything:

and
in the taking in and the tasting of

hidden behind doors with too many windows

I'm wondering if unplanned intrusions or buildings on fire

Could pull me away from seven seasons worth of waiting

Frustrations taken out on lips that taste as good as they've looked

For as long as I've looked at them.

<u>Protective</u>

is the adjective you like to hang on,

Like of your feelings and your heart and all of the other things you claim I'm intent on taking

And you're right

about the taking if not the need

For the word you use to describe the excuses you tell yourself

Warding off advances and eventualities

Putting up a fight better saved

For the tangling coming after

You hang up your favorite word

And relent to one

just

like

this.

You're better to stay away

because it would be six Saturdays before
I'd let you out of the war

we'd call bed

Scratching and clawing and entangling

for all the scratching and clawing and
entangling

it took to land us to land between sheets
in the first place

So please, for the sake of peace and
prosperity

ignore the loaded guns I call longing
glances

save your grenades for boys as half-
beautiful;

Stick to the wars you're equipped to win.

<u>Interlude</u>

I'm at this book signing

Signing books that are better

Than the books I'm surrounded by;

Books about poetry,

Because poetry is hot right now

But not as hot as mine

And I'm going to write

...139, 2

To prove it to you

And the rest of the world

And I'm sorry

It'll take me tearing you apart

for 139 Pages, too

To prove it.

The Ones to Keep You

<u>This section is decidedly smaller</u>

By design and degrees;

Because no one reads a book called

"139 Pages of Pining"

For happy shit.

7 & 7

You're Seagram's and 7-Up

Cocaine and Coffee

...pretty much everything that tastes good and is better for you.

<u>7 & 9</u>

are numbers and initials

and initially

that's all they were and could be;

Circumstances and other terrible words
that start with consonants keeping the
eventuality of

Us

somewhere other than

right here

and

right now

and

right here

and

right now

I'm looking down at the arm with your
initial scratched on it

And I'm pretty fucking thankful

my initial on your little foot

is being scratched on too;

Circumstances going the way of
complications that start with consonants

And leaving eventualities and hidden
meanings to start and stay

the way that tattoo needle promises they
will.

<u>You're Double-Stuffed Oreos</u>

to my inner fat kid;

90 mile per hour run from the cops

to my socially-challenged/misunderstood mid-twenties

Heroin

to my just-wait-till-I'm-successful indulgencies

Yeah, I guess this is my way of saying

You're pretty

and pretty cool.

<u>Us, by the numbers.</u>

I'm 67% schizophrenic
(-and I have the brain
scan to prove it)

23% righteous anger
and whatever's left
is the space to like

Someone like you;

99% pure like that soap
claims to be

1% crazy as fuck
for liking me, too.

"Does this make my ass look fat?"

And the answer is

Yes,

And thank-the-God-I-Don't-Believe-in for it,

Because it's 2018

And baby, your fat ass is, to the eloquent gentleman in me

My Favorite thing about you.

So park it in the passenger seat

And hold on tight;

Despite what everything you've ever read about me has told you,

I swear this won't end the bad my fifty-thousand-four-hundred-sixty-two words printed would beg to differ.

Chicken Soup

ain't got shit on you.

<u>Saturdays are for</u>

Curling on couches

(--outside of football season)

Movie marathons and

Red wine

and

Light sodomy;

and

Driving to destinations

Far away from here and the reality

We want no part of

But spend the majority of days ending in 'y' tethered to.

<u>Sundays are for driving</u>

(--outside of football season)

and back from whatever destination
we ran away to;

back to the reality of shared workplaces
and the secrets we're forced to keep

pent up, round pen,

Horses

let loose on Fridays

Power pushing us down roads

and away from the reality/predicament we
find ourselves in.

<u>Your clothes on the floor</u>

Comfort in ways

The blankets we tangle in

Never could;

The only mess my self-diagnosed OCD can justify

They're a mess

And yet

Less

Than the mess I'll make of

You

Covered in tangled sheets and the mess my love makes

All over you and yet not

The clothes you'll escape in.

Favorite and Four-Letter Words

Stay

and

Next,

respectively.

<u>I'm an acquired taste</u>

admittedly,

Beer to a ten-year-old

Broken wing to a Ballerina,

the kind of maybe-not-sure

that told you to stay away

and got you into this mess,

equal parts

"maybe it's not so bad"

and

"fuck I need to leave."

<u>I'm Bi-Polar, maybe …</u>

Most likely when it comes to the ball of yarn in my head

Most certainly when it comes to
processing
anything that has to do with you

And that smile

And that ass;

Like I need/want/can't-stand-it
Around or over you

So when I apologize for the drama that comes with dating me

I don't apologize

- - get it?

Hotel hallways, weak analogies

I was raised in hotel hallways

More out there than in here

And I'm always sleeping outside

Missing out on the conversations and the kinds of things I suppose one

conventionally keeps behind closed doors

So why not out in the open anyways

If all the world is a stage

And we all have our parts to play

Let me show you what you've been missing

Hiding away under pesky ceilings.

<u>You should have been a boxer.</u>

you move faster

and you hit harder

tip-toeing around the rings we spar in

throwing words and hooks and jabs

and even though you're punching above your weight class

you're winning every round

I'm running out of canvas to circle

before you put me down.

<u>If relationships are like fights</u>

then I've won more than I've lost

(--fuck it, I am a fighter, and I've won more than I've lost)

But I know full well
I'm going to take an L with you

worth the beating and the bruising and the scratching and the blood

black eyes and sore teeth and scarred skin and light head

still swinging for proverbial fences

still pursing for literal kisses

because concussions are fun

and your taste twice as.

I'm no good for you

is today's understatement of the year,

compounded and kissed by the simple fact
that I want you too much to lose you

the way we both know I already kinda *am*

three weeks into something that carries

the weight of seasons comma seven

And I've placed burdens on shoulders slim
as yours

for the totality of the time I've tricked

girls as half-beautiful as you

into believing I'm actually the guy you see
on the poster

less 'as advertised' and more 'hazard:
dangerous road ahead.'

This will end violently

Because that's how it goes

and

Because I guess we've kinda earned it;

Down in flames the way

the great ones always go

Left scarred and fuck that second r

so

scared

And of opening as wide and burning as bad

as skinned knees at seven

But not healing half as well

Thirty years and several layers removed

Going down swinging

For what I hope is the last time,

Running out of flesh left to tear.

Pedestals are Prisons.

just another name,

like 'King of Pop'

for Mike;

Bad

but undeniable just the same.

So I'm still about the placings

(--in case you bothered to read the first one)

but I'm getting better at recognizing the bars pedestals and my placings-on are presenting in patterns,

stripes on shirts I'd prefer stay solid.

You're right at the top,

"Ten Things I Don't Deserve!"

but take anyways,
right above
Skittles from my baby sister when she was seven
and

Everything,

leaving you with nothing

save the promises I break when I promise I'm worth the love I've spent considerable time taking.

<u>You're distractingly pretty and suitcase small</u>

Too pretty for pieces,

which is why the protector in me

prefers you stay in situations, safe

So stay

because it's late and I've got knives

and I promise you're safer here

than the *anywhere out there*

I'll tell you just about anything

to keep you from.

...

Yeah, the danger's more

Out there

than

In here

and when you look into my eyes

the fact that you believe

makes you the victim we both kinda
understand you're about to be.

I guess that's why they call it the blues

Said somebody much better at this than me,

And I only see red on days without you in them

So consider time spent charity

Medicine for a breaking, slowly soul

And keep the prescription on refill,

because running out is a crawl to crimson

And I'm dead out of anything but you.

I like spending time with You

is code

for something much more

something that starts with

I

and ends in

You

and, just so you know...

...I like spending time with You, too.

What happens when wine

doesn't taste as good when it's not together?

<u>Editors and English Teachers</u> loved me

Mothers and Fathers, not so much

And you'll end up somewhere in the middle

After the first words about you

Bleed into the ones after

Once you realize the honey

Stops at honeyed words

And that the guy writing them

Presents well and preserves poorly.

You're four feet, one hundred miles away:

Head down and typing furiously on a phone better suited for sending furiously typed texts to me

Sending someone else the somethings I've been missing

So please, put away the distractions

you pretend to distract yourself with,

Focus on the features that landed you in trouble in the first place

and acknowledge that spelling out the things I'm not can't fill

me and the holes my personality punched

<u>I like you more than sushi</u>

--so a whole fucking lot

And I need you more than

-corrective eye surgery

-rehab

-Jesus

And the litany of things my doctor and my mother tell me I need;

taking the lead with big eyes and big hair and that ass,

Priority Number One, even on the nights the whiskey and my rampant alcoholism beg to differ.

<u>Interlude</u>

I'm horrible at the following;

-paying attention

-math

-dancing

-adult life

-you

However, one of the two things I'm good at

Is writing *this*,

And this shit is popular now

Bookstores full of poetry books that absolutely fucking suck

But are more popular

So do me a favor

Tell your friends this one is about you

--because it kinda is

--and tell your friends to pick up a copy

Because it's better than the shit they're reading, too.

The Ones to Lose You

For such a cute voice

You sure make hurtful sounds.

<u>I like you more</u>

Than the things I really like

Cocaine

And

Coffee

And

The other wonderful things that come from

The magical made-up land you come from

And I'll write my next-best book about it

So stay tuned

In the meantime

Here's to the hurt I'm about to

Blowing this because I tend to

Having read the end to the book I'll write about you.

You're on your way out the door

Literally

And

Figuratively

And I figure

It's for the best

Because I pushed you here

And

I'm too

Tired/stubborn/stupid

To admit that this may be the

First of what admittedly might

Be a

Season of bad ideas.

Mine

And

Stay

Are the most powerful words in the English language?

And they hate each other

Because they know they *can't*

make you do either or be,

Gone

and

Long

left and pretty fucking powerful, too.

Tiny Eventualities.

I always kinda figured I'd end up here

Prison, real or imagined

Stealing cars and hearts

for far too many years to get away with it

the way I was until you

Put me here

And the bars might be metaphorical or they might not be metaphorical

but no better off

having known we both saw this coming

and couldn't end up anywhere than

here

and where you leave me

the way you should

to the cage I knew I'd find

not quite the man it takes to avoid tiny
eventualities.

<u>I hurl words like weapons</u>

Because yours hurt too,
marriage
and
kids
daggers, parried with

single
And
Never

the words that won the war
and left me alone
that maybe this book and these words
kinda make me have to be

<u>You woulda been perfect</u>

a partner and a pal and a shoulder and a soul

but

perfect isn't quite the ending I figured I deserve

and so

I had to sell you short

like the short I said I fell in love with

five-foot-nothing and standing taller now,

the all alone I freed you to.

AZ

You're 3,475 miles away

literally,

and maybe double that

leaving things the way we leave them.

And still I figure

you're the best/worst thing for me

black hair and blue eyes

leaving me the kinda colors

you backing off

has beat me down to.

So I'll love you from the distance

the miles were kind enough to create

settle for the knowing

that proximity is poison

when two people exchange particles

with the fury and the fire

we exchanged ours.

And yeah, I love you

and yeah, I always will

but you should stay in your corner

warm and dry and safe

and leave the winter and the cold

to someone better suited

for the black fingers and blue toes

your winter wake wound up wounding when you left.

I'm fucking you

And over

And you're doing your best to stay the pretty that got you into trouble in the first place,

Finishing somewhere other than the

First place

I promised when I lied,

First of several you put up a good fight fighting

Right before the fucking

--and over!

began.

I guess you could say

"<u>I messed up</u>"

is an oversimplification, *kinda*

Like saying that

turning out to really be

everything I said

foreshadowed

promised

I was and am

is a surprise.

So

Surprise!

I'm an asshole and a liar and a bamboozler

--and not just because it's my favorite word

but because I promise I'm the same hopeless case

I was when I promised

and you made the mistake of loving me anyways.

80 Pages in,

and I'm running out of steam;

and it's not like

I haven't hurt the 59 women I need to have hurt

To fill the rest of the pages I promised;

but fuck if writing down my celebrated list of failures

hasn't left me a little uninspired

--so heaven forgive the next number I call

In the name of finishing this book

Sorry in advance

for the next page

--the first of a few

likely about you.

You're better than me

at math and polite conversation and at

this

--the whole 'love' thing

and maybe it's because of this that I string you along,

pretending really hard, (because that's all I've ever been really good at)

when I look you in the eyes and promise that

No

I won't hurt you again and

No

I'm not hurting you right now

Latest in a series of lies I might maybe lie myself into believing.

I'm losing you on rerun

--meaning I've seen this movie before;

and pressing pause won't change the ending

So spoiler alert(!)

the car crash is coming

and you're going to be left a little worse for wear

wearing that t-shirt I gave you

on the first Wednesday since the wreckage

telling yourself that having your name in the credits

means you'll be remembered when the screen goes black.

Roses to Rust

I'll turn roses to rust
on my 'left out in the rain' shit
real good at ruining
pretty little things like you
And writing clever words about it

After the hurt has gone
The way of the pedals

Put down on to the floor
Of the cute little cars

You and the other ones run away in

Little Johnny Reiner

I lost a fight in the seventh grade

when Johnny Reiner kicked me in the balls

--and this kinda feels like that,

laying on the playground and praying

that my poor little grade seven balls grow back

After the metaphorical kicking

your up and leaving

has left me laying in.

Tell your parents

And your dignity

And your goddamned dog

And our unborn child

And your Saturday night complacencies

I'm sorry

For the future(s) I've freed

And you're welcome

For the renewed patience

And restored sanity.

I'm at least every cliché

You're right about that,

and

'Danger'

tattooed on my forehead

is about the only tattoo I don't have;

Covering up tiny insecurities and superficial flaws

with tiny little cartoon angels and demons

to represent the saving I need and the devil I am

Coming as advertised when that tiny little
voice tells you

Runaway

the way these words are trying to.

<u>...because 'Gilbert' isn't a sexy town name.</u>

You're close to Tempe,
One 'r' short of
Temper

--close to describing you too,
and how you react to my inability to
act on the promises I promised you.

And maybe I was too scared to tell you

You scare me

At least twice as beautiful

As the beautiful I'm used to
Three hours behind

Bit ahead in absolutely everything else
Already realizing you've got the potential
To get the best of me,

Hiding up North and under blankets

Ruining the chance to ruin my bed

And the blankets I could have been under
with you, too.

You don't fall

back or forward

down there;

So if Daylight Savings Time can't fool you

what chance did a fool like me have

You saw right through

the me I tried to be

because I really really wanted to;

Focused instead on the man I am

maybe more importantly,

The man I'm not

So I see you're happy

and I am, for you

Way up here, three or four ahead

depending on the season

Some seasons since you failed to fall for
me.

<u>...in light of explanations, here's one that hurts</u>

I aged better than most of the girls in the books I wrote.

And it's about the only thing I'm not sorry for

Because if you spent any kinda time with me

You were fair game

for the words I wrote to wash off the sins I probably sinned but blamed

any-all of you temporarily foolish enough to stay

And eventually smart enough to leave

me and the pages I probably wrote to get back at you.

I create monsters

and then cut them loose.

<u>Weekends go by</u>

And you're anywhere else

and tonight's a Saturday

and that same bar is holding you down

the way I used to;

So while you're collecting attention

I'm catching the kinds of feels

it takes to write this,

One more page

Until I'm both done and famous

and everywhere else

But that same bar

That'll still be holding you down.

I'll miss the nights

with just you in them;

the ones with wine

and wasted time

the ones with drugs

and the sleep drugs bring

holding you

way back when

the only thing we missed

was the alarm in the morning

and ruined

was just the sheets.

Here's a hint:

When I say

"I'm fine"

I'm really

really

Not

and

the way your breath stops

when you walk away

--just that little bit?

That's something other than the lies your lips move to make

when you tell yourself you're fine, too.

I'm Over

Six feet tall

(--at least that's what I tell myself)

and

I'm Over

that last Super Bowl

(--because there's always next season, until there's not)

and

Of all the things I'm really really over

I'm Over

telling myself and at least everyone who asks

That yes,

I'm Over You.

<u>Patterns are for bad shirts</u>

and my relationship behaviors, apparently

And thank you for giving it a shot anyways,

Three years of trying to save someone so clearly drowning

while treading water too

coming out (mostly) unscathed

maybe a little wet and out of breath

But much

much

much

Better off

and a stronger swimmer with better fashion sense, too.

<u>I wrote four of these</u>

In the time it took you
To finish that glass of wine

So here's to the next one
-- I'll race you
Put it to your lips
Before I put it to
the page;

Both chasing this away in our own way
And I'll let you guess which is more
self-destructive.

<u>Losing you is the only thing worse</u>

than watching Tom lose 'Bowls;

and I realize that references like *this*

date this a little bit,

But it's because we dated

a little bit

that these words are here in the first place, at all

So I'm getting older, like Tom, and it's sad

because I've only got a few big plays left in me, too

the losing likely to make the next play even more reckless

Than the reckless that initially attracted

and eventually lost

you.

I play with fire

the way you played with Barbie;

stole cars and hearts and big screen TVs

while you were stealing candy and learning how to count

and you can count, blessings and more

that I'm the gone those items were

from the places I stole them;

the bad my tattoos told you

tracing them in my bed and for the first time

my latest/greatest heist landed you there

back when the fire was from the candle and the look in your eyes and only.

<u>Gambling isn't good to me</u>

But I'll bet I'm better

Than whoever is wasting all your time
these days.

As if

Running out of time

isn't the most tragically romantic fun a breaking, slowly heart can have.

Yeah, you're the best I'll ever have

Drake before the come-up;

And I use future tense

Because I've already written the end

to this particular book;

So looking forward

to nights without you in them

is about all I have to look forward to,

and a hell of a lot more fun than looking back

Nights curled on couches

not half the fun now

Holding whiskey instead of

and waiting on mornings

colder than May ought to be.

<u>I don't miss the hair</u>

Fucking everywhere in my apartment

after Fucking everywhere in my apartment;

And I'm still finding

Fucking hair

Everywhere

Silver strand ghosts

Hanging around and longer

Than you had sense to.

If "<u>Don't Let Me Push You Away</u>"

was the homework

then I failed you like that Grade 10 math

the first three times I took that driving test

and, I guess,

any hope in hell of being happy

the way you lied when you promised we could be.

Saudade

is my new favourite word and

well worth a Google;

it's the way I feel

about the distance I caused

too much time looking up weird words

with meanings

I wouldn't need to worry about

if I'd just closed my book and

paid attention.

Tell me

The things I lack;

Common sense

and

Self-Respect

and

Dignity

and

Everything you tell me

but the things you can't;

Penis size

and

Stamina

and

A voracious and all-consuming desire to consume you

Even after the things you tell me I lack

Running the way you should

and

Out of breath, too.

I'd rather

-skydive

-wrangle poisonous snakes

-visit my Grandmother

than move my lips to mouth

I'm sorry

the way I'm supposed to;

So here's everything but,

and for the behaviors

that pushed you out of the metaphorical planes

I'm left to consider jumping out of

legs willing to move when lips don't.

In your life

You're in love with a couple of things

and leaving

is one of them

and unfortunately for me

the other one won.

<u>Today I almost threw out</u>

The last of the things you bought for our old fridge;

Yeah, those make-them-yourself pickles were fucked

Until I saw how empty those shelves would be

And the whole "fend for myself" thing kicked up

And maybe I missed you

And so the preservatives-I-hope

Preserve;

Turns out the 'Best Before' date was on everything else.

<u>In your defense</u>

You thought 'Chinese Democracy' was worth the wait;

So even though you went from

This New One

to

That Old One

The memory of your musical taste

And your taste-taste

Earn you a page here on Volume Two

Way at the back, but still somewhat relevant

Like that band we listened to on days when the writing concerned you and only.

I thought about you once

While writing

Wrote about sunshine and summer days

And some other sappy shit

And then I thought about you a little more

tore that shit up

Wrote the pages with pretty bad pretty words in them

To maybe justify the fact I had to search my memory

For time with you I'll never spend

Present tense

And maybe a little bit because of the words I just wrote about you.

Interlude

I'm on store shelves

Alphabetical under 'Amazing'

Presenting better

Than the me you get to know

/deal with

And if a modicum of success

Has me insufferable

Imagine the nightmare time spent will be

When the book about you

Hits shelves beside books by lesser writers and better humans.

The Ones About Me (--and my epic and monumental shortcomings)

Of all the Irrational Animals,

Apologetic Alphas

are the fucking worst.

--so, sorry ;)

Inconsistently Awful

is amongst my favorite
of the names you called me;

Well-earned and spoken
more consistently
than the times I was
Consistently

Absent,

Emotionally and
finally,
Physically.

I write Volumes

so I don't have to speak them.

<u>I've been writing more</u>

And thinking less

About
And of

You
And the things that both push the pen
And out the door.

<u>I'm worse on the weekend</u>

which sucks for every Sunday

outside Football season

and for every girl

stupid enough to believe in sleepless Saturdays

or in me, at all.

So apologies for wasted ends

and worried weeks

knowing *next* is five or less away

and the whiskey or the season will stain
me

the way last Sunday stained you.

<u>I need Jesus</u>
and church on Sunday
and a pretty big bath

if I'm gonna wash away
the sins of someone else

Staining my lips and my
breath and the conscience
buried beneath

The word that come out
of my dirty mouth

When I tell you I'm not
the sinner

My sins would so clearly
beg to differ.

Just the right amount of

Despair and Determination

And I can write the kind of shit

To make your mother blush

And your daddy write me off

And if I practiced what I preach

I'd be the locked away I probably should be

Stealing futures unjaded

By horrible experiences with bad boys

Responsible for the jading

Since back when Oprah was fat

For the first time.

Irascible, but justifiably so.

I'll justify

Bad behavior and poor judgement

As job requirement

I'll call

Relentless stubbornness and an overwhelming desire to make my poorly-researched point

Necessary qualities for an introverted, introspective troubadour

And

I'm irascible

(--worth a google)

Because it makes the writing better

So when I call my bad behavior

Bones

And for my next book

Take it on the chin

Like the left I won't throw

Better at wounding with words

And childish temperament

Selfish and arrogant and petty and small

And (--thanks for buying this book!)

Celebrated for it.

Dressing pretty

Doesn't discount dirt

Hidden under nails and years

And

Poor

is just my judgement, now

Having fought hard to keep
"I'm from here"
the kind of secret I tend to,

--the kind that kills pretty, shows scars.

Motivation:

Backbeats

Bass Drums

&

Bad Words.

My Momma's Not Gonna Like This One

But fuck it, there's only about two pages that pass

Her rose-coloured-glasses version of the son I'm not;

So once this sells
The way it should
I'm going to buy a bobber
(Bonneville)
And a ball
(8)
And I'll either be super inspired
Or
Super dead
By the time it's time for 139,3

I go for girls

with Sugar Baby Tendencies

Questionable asses and ethics

--like maybe real, maybe not

But the kind of girls I go for

are the kind of fun

that encourage the kinds of behavior

you're benefitting from, reading This Book

and the next one

about the next one

I swear

--this time for real!

that hurt me the hardest.

I'm on my Marcus Aurelius shit

Meditating

On the kinds of things a guy like me meditates on;

Thing like girls

And fights

And fights with girls

--the kinds of things

That pick up the pen

On days I'd rather not;

Write the things that my destroyed sense of self-worth would rather I didn't

--the kinds of things on the very next page.

I'm less about half-naked selfies

and more about half-naked soul-I-swear-I-still-have-one exposing;

and while my followers on the 'Gram might appreciate the former

You and a very small portion of the population

kinda digs the latent hopelessness of the latter.

<u>So can we call these lyrics?</u>

I've got too much testosterone for poems

Too much withering insecurity for
free-verse

Too much false cleverness for anything
remembering honesty

My Daddy isn't overly proud of me

and I kinda don't blame him

the sum of his son is several thousand
fucks and the words surrounding them;

pages and pages to apologize for potential
had and unrealized

brain damage and bad decisions where
scholarships and sanctity used to/should be

before marriage/kids/settle became the bad
words

and the bad words just became common.

I'm suicidal before coffee

and a little on Sundays

curmudgeonly earlier than I have any right to be

a rascal and a scoundrel and a bamboozler and a good person before six and only

The Patron Saint of Sometimes, still

and yet somehow I fall

into situations like this;

working hard to explain my lesser qualities

in the face of someone

foolish enough to stand in my wake

brave enough to hang around

long enough to prove myself right.

If my books are albums, then this shit is an EP

More punch per page, and these are the pages that punch back,

leaving me wounded and more exposed

than a book about some guy I pretend isn't me

I'll bury this one too, ten years done before advertised on sale

I'll blush when you bring it up, sign it different when you ask

Like I'm proud of it, I guess,

hide from it like the feelings

I tell myself aren't there

And then tell the world different when they read every single word after this one.

<u>Friends and Family Members</u>

Aren't crazy about this one

Like maybe I'm the kind of

Crazy

These pages kinda make me out to be

Or maybe I'm misunderstood

And it's one of those

As a Fox

jams;

Either way, I'm the topic of conversation

139 Pages should have painted you to be;

And I'll take it on the chin

Because the next one

--the one really about you?

Is 139 Pages away

From starting a whole new conversation.

138 Pages of Pining

Doesn't have quite the same kick

And so, while I swear this isn't just some half-assed attempt to pad the page count

You can't blame me

If the vein hasn't been tapped

And the blood it takes

(Of the sweat and tears too)

Isn't run dry

Running around

The troubled mind it takes

To pine for 138 Pages and………………………………

Last One

And I've got nothing clever left

So in closing

Just let me say

Thank You

For the hurt it took

To be this brave.

www.ingramcontent.com/pod-product-compliance
Lightning Source LLC
Chambersburg PA
CBHW070045120526
44589CB00035B/2328